Animal Neighbors

Mouse

Stephen Savage

PowerKiDS press.

New York

Published in 2009 by The Rosen Publishing Group Inc.
29 East 21st Street, New York, NY 10010

First Edition

Commissioning Editor: Victoria Brooker
Produced by Nutshell Media
Editor: Polly Goodman
Designer: Tim Mayer
Illustrator: Jackie Harland

Library of Congress Cataloging-in-Publication Data

Savage, Stephen, 1965-
Mouse / Stephen Savage. — 1st ed.
p. cm. — (Animal neighbors)
Includes index.
ISBN 978-1-4358-4990-7 (library binding)
ISBN 978-1-4042-4567-9 (paperback)
ISBN 978-1-4042-4579-2 (6-pack)
1. Mice—Juvenile literature. I. Title.
QL737.R666S37 2009
599.35'3—dc22
                                        2008005414

Picture acknowledgements
FLPA 7 (Martin Withers), 9, 10, 13, 20 (Jurgen & Christine Sohns), 24 (By Silvestris), 28 right, 28 bottom
(Jurgen & Christine Sohns); naturepl.com 27 (Georgette Douwma); NHPA Title page, 19, 21 (Stephen
Dalton), 22 (Joe Blossom), 23 (Ant Photo Library), 25 (Manfred Danegger), 28 left (Joe Blossom); Oxford
Scientific Films Cover (Rodger Jackman), 6 (Michael Fogden), 8 (Tony Bomford), 11 (Zig Leszczynski/AA),
12 (Kathie Atkinson), 14 (OSF), 15, 16 (Rodger Jackman), 17 (Satoshi Kuribayashi), 26 (Rodger
Jackman), 28 top (Tony Bomford).

Manufactured in China

Contents

Meet the Mouse

Mice are small, agile rodents. They have adapted to almost every habitat, from fields and forests, to deserts, towns, and cities. Mice live everywhere in the world apart from the polar regions.

This book looks at the house mouse and why it is the most widespread of all the mouse species.

▲ This shows the size of a house mouse compared to an adult human hand.

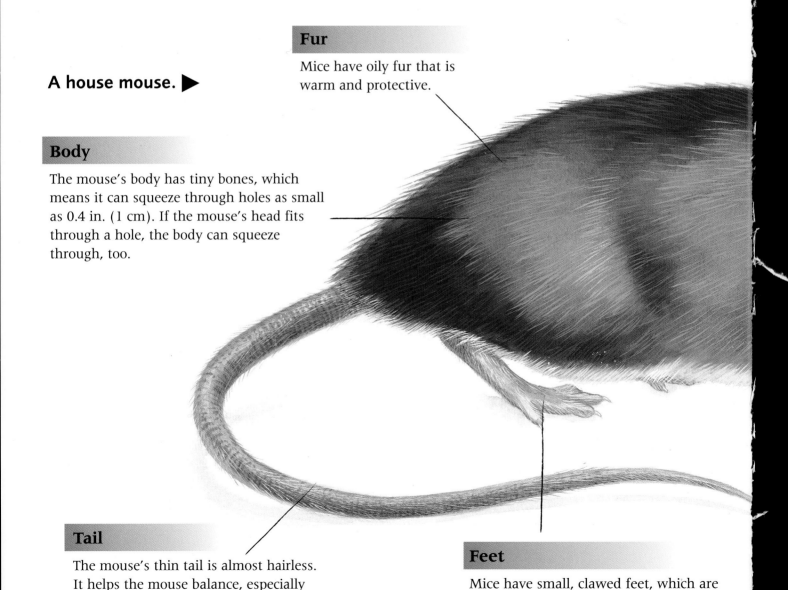

A house mouse. ▶

Fur

Mice have oily fur that is warm and protective.

Body

The mouse's body has tiny bones, which means it can squeeze through holes as small as 0.4 in. (1 cm). If the mouse's head fits through a hole, the body can squeeze through, too.

Tail

The mouse's thin tail is almost hairless. It helps the mouse balance, especially when standing on its hind legs.

Feet

Mice have small, clawed feet, which are ideal for running and climbing.

4

Ears

Mice have large ears and an excellent sense of hearing, which is their main sense for detecting danger.

MOUSE FACTS

The house mouse's scientific name is *Mus musculus*, from the Latin word *musculus* meaning "little mouse."

The word *mouse* comes from the word for "thief" in Sanskrit, an ancient Indian language.

Male mice are known as bucks, females as does, and young mice as pups.

The house mouse's body is about 3.5 in. (9 cm) long without the tail. The tail is almost as long as the body. Adult house mice weigh about 1 oz. (30 g).

Eyes

Mice have poor eyesight and they cannot see things in color. Since they move around mostly in the dark, mice rely more on their whiskers to find their way around.

Nose

The mouse has a good sense of smell for finding food. It also uses smell to recognize other mice from their scent-marks.

Teeth

Like all rodents, mice have chisel-shaped teeth to gnaw food, which continue to grow throughout their lives. The teeth must be ground down by gnawing on hard objects to stop them from growing too long.

Whiskers

Whiskers grow from sensitive pits on the mouse's face. They help the mouse to find its way through tunnels and around its territory in the dark.

5

The Mouse Family

Mice belong to the largest group of mammals, the rats and mice family. Scientists call this group the "mouselike group of rodents." It includes various species of mice, rats, voles, gerbils, hamsters, and lemmings.

All mouselike rodents are mouse-shaped, but they vary greatly in body size, and the size and shape of their ears, tail, and feet. Many dig burrow systems where they live in colonies.

▼ **This southern grasshopper mouse is eating a freshly killed harvest mouse.**

Most mice are omnivores that feed on seeds, insects, and carrion, but a few species are carnivores. The grasshopper mouse lives in the grasslands of the United States. Apart from grasshoppers, it also eats scorpions and even other mice, some of which are bigger than itself.

The tiny harvest mouse has a clever way of hiding from predators. It builds nests attached to the stalks of grasses and crops, 12–40 in. (30–100 cm) above the ground, where it retreats in times of danger. The dusky hopping mouse from Australia escapes danger by bounding along on its hind legs like a kangaroo.

◀ A harvest mouse peers out from its nest, which is perched up above the ground.

Birth and Growing Up

In the countryside, most house mice are born between March and October, when there is the most food available. House mice that live in towns and cities can be born at almost any time of the year.

Before she gives birth, a pregnant doe will prepare a nest in a warm, dark place. This could be under a garage roof, in a storage box in an attic, or in the corner of a barn. If it is her first litter, the doe will have to build the nest from scratch. But she may already have a nest from previous litters.

A litter of newborn ▶ pups huddle together to keep warm while their mother forages for food.

MOUSE PUPS

Newborn pups are about 1.2 in. (30 mm) long and weigh about 0.009 oz. (2.5 mg).

The average sized litter is five or six pups, although a doe can give birth to as many as thirteen.

The young pups are born pink, blind, and completely helpless. They are hairless except for the tiny whiskers on their faces, and their eyes and ears are tightly closed. The newborn pups have to rely on their mother for food and protection. She cleans and suckles them several times a day, only leaving the nest to find food. When she returns to the nest, the pups recognize their mother by her smell.

Mouse pups grow rapidly. By the time they are 10 days old, they are covered in fur. Their eyes and ears open when they are 14 days old.

▼ A doe suckles her fully furred pups.

Early days

Between 2 and 3 weeks old, the young mice begin to make short trips from their nest and explore their surroundings. The pups start to learn the skills they will need to survive on their own, such as finding their own food, learning to be secretive, and avoiding danger.

By 3–4 weeks old, the young mice are fully weaned and leave the nest for good. By now, their mother is pregnant again.

GROOMING

Keeping clean is a regular activity for mice, and a skill that young mice need to learn. Mice groom their fur with their teeth and scratch themselves with their hind feet. They use their front paws to "wash" their face and their teeth for nibbling fur. Mice also groom each other with their teeth to show friendship.

▼ Two young house mice nibble at a tasty blackberry.

As it leaves the nest where it was born, the young mouse faces many dangers and most do not survive their first year. Apart from the threat of predators, such as cats, foxes, and birds of prey, young mice are driven away by adult mice, who are often aggressive toward the young. The greater the number of mice living in a place, the farther the young mouse will have to travel from where it was born.

◄ Many young house mice are eaten by predators, such as this long-eared owl.

Habitat and Home

In towns and cities, there are lots of places for mice to live. They make their homes in holes and cracks in walls, buildings, and bridges. Mice often live in houses, either in the space between the walls, under floorboards, or in attics and basements. In toolsheds and garages, they live among cardboard boxes and flowerpots. Although some mice live permanently in houses, others only enter homes in the winter, when they are looking for food and warmth.

▼ Storage jars make useful stepping stones for this mouse exploring a kitchen.

Elsewhere in towns and cities, parks, warehouses, and railroad stations provide shelter and food for house mice. In zoos and wildlife parks, house mice live in enclosures alongside rhinoceroses, monkeys, and other animals.

In the countryside, house mice often live in farm buildings such as barns. They are especially common on farms where crops are grown and grain is stored. Some mice live in nearby fields, hedges, and derelict buildings.

▼ This house mouse lives in a field of corn, which provides its favorite food.

▲ A doe gathers
scraps of material
to make a nest.

The nest

Mice build their nests in places that are dark and
warm, safe from the prying eyes of predators. The
doe shreds a variety of available materials with her
teeth and weaves them together with the help of her
front feet to make the nest. Mouse nests are roughly
ball-shaped and about 4 in. (10 cm) in diameter.

Urban mice use paper, sacks, clothing, roof
insulation, string, and other soft materials to make
their nests. Favorite nest sites include storage boxes,
drawers, underneath kitchen appliances, and inside
the upholstery of furniture.

In the countryside, the nest is made from more natural materials, such as dried grass, leaves, and hay. Nests are made in farm buildings, bales of hay, and even underneath hedges. Occasionally, house mice build a tunnel system or make a nest in another animal's disused burrow.

COLD HOME

The most unusual nest site for house mice is in a cold store, living at temperatures of 14 °F (–10 °C). In almost total darkness, both males and females tunnel and feed on the frozen meat. A nest is made for rearing young using the meat's burlap wrapping. Mice that live in these cold conditions become larger and heavier. Their fat helps to keep them warm.

Once it is built, each mouse nest will probably be used to raise several litters of pups. Does sometimes nest together and help to nurse each other's pups. This is most likely with does that are related.

▼ This house mouse has made its nest in some old stuffing in a workshop.

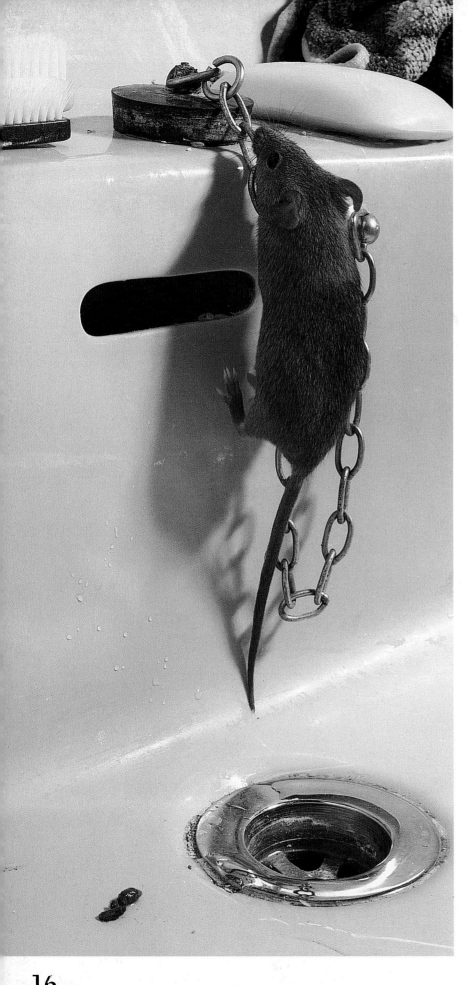

Territory

House mice live in small groups containing several does and one dominant male. Each group lives within a home range, or territory, which is usually no more than 9.8 yards (9 meters) in diameter.

The mice in each group scent-mark the borders of their territory with urine, so that other mice know the territory belongs to them. The dominant male then defends it from intruders. Rural mice are more defensive of their territory than those living in towns and cities.

Mice memorize the pathways in their territory and use the same routes every night. They find their way in the dark by touch, using the long whiskers on their nose.

◀ Mice are excellent climbers. This one is using a plug chain to climb out of a slippery sink.

House mice are nocturnal animals, which means they are mostly active at night. However, they can usually be heard scuttling around behind a wall during the day. A mouse can leap up to 12 in. (30 cm) from the ground and climb up a brick wall. It can run along the tops of pipes and electrical cables and drop 2.7 yards (2.5 meters) to the floor.

◀ A house mouse leaps using its powerful back legs while the tail is used for balance.

COMMUNICATION

Mice can often be heard making squeaking sounds, but they make many calls that we do not hear because they are too quiet for our level of hearing. These quieter calls are social messages to nearby mice, or for calling a lost pup. The calls travel short distances only, which prevents predators from hearing them.

Food and Foraging

Mice are omnivores. They eat parts of plants, seeds, fruit, insects, and carrion. Occasionally, they eat worms and fungi. Rural house mice feed on cereal crops and cereal grain in grain stores.

▼ House mice are at the center of several food chains. (The illustrations are not to scale.)

Mouse food chain

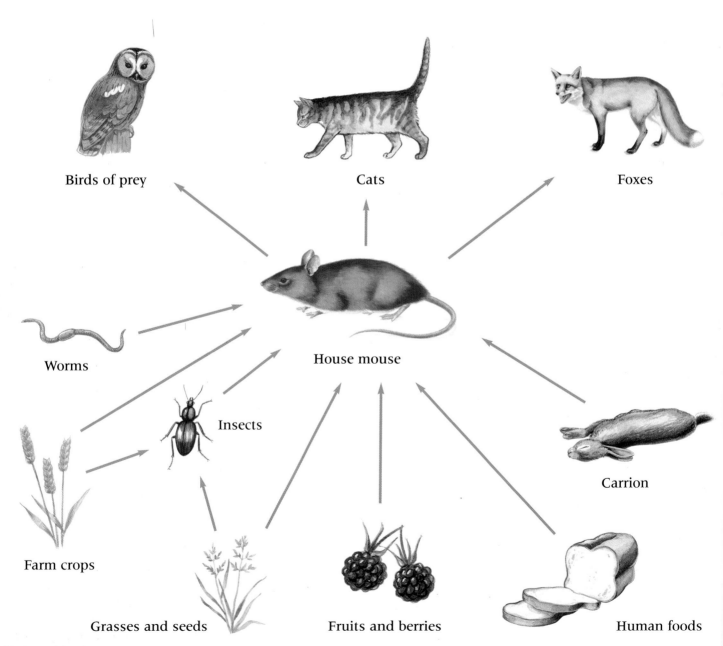

Birds of prey

Cats

Foxes

Worms

House mouse

Insects

Carrion

Farm crops

Grasses and seeds

Fruits and berries

Human foods

The house mouse's favorite food is grain, or food containing grain, such as bread and cookies. Mice will eat almost any human food, although unlike the cartoon mice we see on television, cheese is not one of their favorites. Urban mice often eat foods high in protein or fat, such as bacon and butter, or high in sugar, such as chocolate and sweets. These foods provide lots of energy and fat for warmth.

◀ **This house mouse has eaten its way into a loaf of bread.**

Foraging

Since much of the mouse's activity takes place at night or in dark places, it relies on its sense of smell to find food. Mice have a good sense of smell and taste, and they are very good at recognizing and remembering foods that they like or dislike. Any new foods they encounter are approached with caution.

Mice always seem to be busy looking for food, but they do not need to eat much. A single mouse eats only about 0.1 ounce (3 grams) of food per day. In people's houses, most food is nibbled and discarded, before the mouse moves on to another item. This means that more food is damaged than actually eaten.

◀ This agile mouse has climbed down a rope to reach a hanging joint of meat.

▲ When mice gnaw through electric cables like this one, it can be dangerous for both the mouse and the household.

Water

House mice drink water regularly if it is available, but they can survive without drinking because they use the small amounts of water that are present in their food. This is probably an ability inherited from their Asian ancestors, who had fewer towns and cities to get water, food, and shelter. If mice do not get enough water, however, it reduces their ability to breed.

UNUSUAL FOODS

Apart from human food, house mice also eat some very strange items, such as plaster, glue, soap, candles, and wood. They probably eat these items simply because they are something to nibble and they are attracted to them by their smell. Mice can do a lot of damage chewing through electrical wiring, damaging furniture and stored items, such as books and documents.

Finding a Mate

When they are 5 weeks old, does are ready to mate. Bucks usually have to wait until they are 10 weeks old, because they have to set up their own territory first. This is because does will only mate with the dominant male of the group. After mating, the buck leaves the doe and plays no part in rearing the young.

▼ A group of mice may start with just a male and female.

The pups are born about 20 days after mating. This, together with the young age that mice start mating, is why house mice breed so successfully. A doe gives birth every three to four weeks and can have up to ten litters a year.

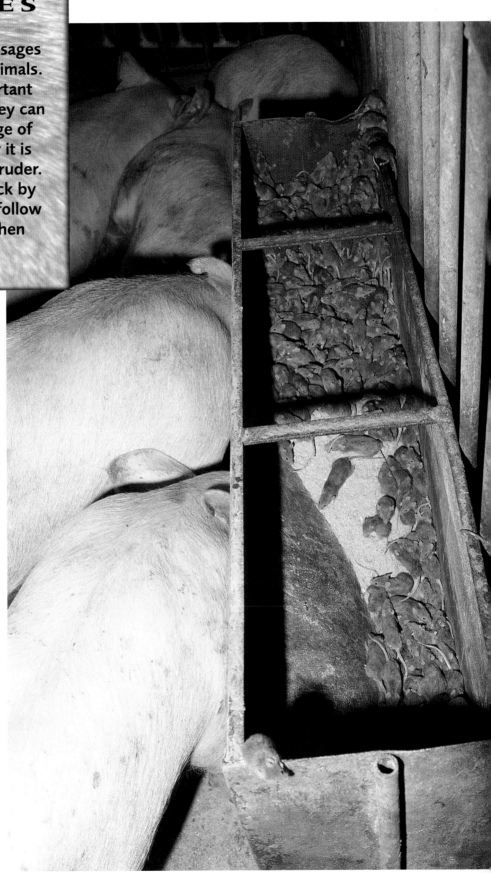

PHEROMONES

Pheromones are chemical messages sent out from the bodies of animals. These messages are an important part of a mouse's daily life. They can be used to tell the sex and age of another mouse, and whether it is from the same group or an intruder. A buck can avoid another buck by detecting its pheromones, or follow the pheromones of a doe when looking for a mate.

▶ A plague of hundreds of mice in a commercial piggery in Australia.

Sometimes the number of mice in an area can become very high, which causes an increase in fighting and squabbles between bucks. Overcrowding can cause some of the females in a group to temporarily or even permanently stop producing young. This helps to prevent the mice numbers increasing faster than the amount of space and food available.

Threats

Mice face threats from many predators. In the countryside, they are important prey for a wide variety of animals. Owls, kestrels, and other birds of prey swoop down on them in fields. Foxes and badgers hunt mice in woodlands, digging up their nests or catching the young as they first leave the nest. Two similar predators, the weasel and the larger stoat, both prey on house mice. The mouse's only defenses are caution, moving around under cover, and being quick when they are detected.

▼ A kestrel swoops down on a house mouse just outside the entrance to its nest.

A major predator of mice is the domestic cat. Many people think of cats as the mouse's worst enemy. Although some cats are very good at catching mice, others would rather just curl up in front of the fire. Some cats, such as farm cats, are not kept as pets but for their ability to catch mice.

▼ Domestic cats often kill mice because they have a strong hunting instinct.

DOMESTIC CATS

Early civilizations domesticated wild cats to catch mice. It is thought that the Phoenicians, who lived on the Mediterranean coast about 3,000 years ago, brought the first domesticated cats to Europe on cargo ships in about 900 BC. They were probably kept on the ships to catch mice. The Romans introduced cats to Britain by about AD 300, when they occupied part of Britain.

People and mice

The mouse's worst enemy is people. Sometimes house mice live behind a wall and hardly ever enter the main parts of a house. But most mice will forage in kitchens and other parts of the house, taking advantage of the way we store food and trash.

Mice not only eat our foods, they contaminate it by nibbling and leaving droppings, making it unfit to eat. They can also carry diseases, especially in their urine. On farms, mice can damage food kept for livestock. For these reasons, people have waged war on the house mouse for almost as long as mice have lived with people.

▲ Mice have been a pest ever since people started growing crops, especially after harvesting, when grain is stored.

A variety of traps and poisons are used to kill mice. Poisoned grain is left in places for mice to find, but this only works if the mice eat enough of it. House mice have a good memory for tastes and will avoid any foods that taste bad. Also, many mice have become immune to poisons, so they are not always a successful killer. Some people believe that mice should be caught using harmless traps and released away from houses rather than killing them.

▼ Some house mice have learned to eat the cheese without setting off the mousetrap.

LIFESPAN

Mice can live for up to 3 years in the wild. However, few will live for more than a year, and only one or two mice from each litter are likely to survive long enough to become adults. The mouse's lifespan depends on its habitat, which can affect its chances of survival. Mice kept as pets or bred in laboratories can live up to 6 years old.

Mouse Life Cycle

1 Newborn mice are blind, deaf, and naked. An average litter will have five or six pups.

2 Ten days after birth, the pups are covered in fur. Their eyes and ears open when they are 14 days old.

5 A doe can produce her first litter at the age of 5 weeks. Bucks have to wait until they can secure a territory, usually after the age of 10 weeks.

4 At 3–4 weeks, the young mice leave the nest fully weaned. The female mouse may now be pregnant again.

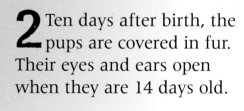

3 At about 18 days old, the young mice leave the nest for the first time and start to forage for food.

Mouse Clues

Look for the following clues to help you find signs of a mouse:

Nest
Shredded paper or other materials may be a sign that mice are nesting nearby. The nest itself will usually be out of sight, but one may be found in an airing cupboard, or boxes in an attic or a garage.

Gnawing
Look for signs of gnawing on wooden objects, such as boxes and furniture, especially where things are stored out of the way. Teeth marks are small and usually appear lighter than the rest of the wood. Sawdust may also be visible.

Droppings
Mouse droppings are found along trails frequently used by mice. They are small, black, and rod-shaped, with pointed ends.

Urine
Urine is deposited as scent trails. Sometimes urine pillars form in special places within a mouse's territory. These are a mixture of urine, grease, dirt, and sometimes droppings.

Sounds
Mice can be quite noisy. You may hear gnawing, scratching, and even scampering behind a wall. Mice also make a squeaking call.

Smell
Mice have a musky smell, particularly the males. Places where mice urinate frequently may also smell, as do the urine pillars.

Footprints
Mice have five toes on their back feet but only four toes on their front feet. A small drag mark where the tail touches the ground may also be visible behind the footprints.

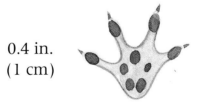

0.4 in. (1 cm)

Front foot

0.7 in. (1.8 cm)

Hind foot

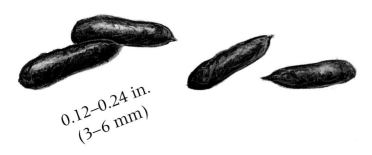

0.12–0.24 in. (3–6 mm)

Glossary

buck A male mouse. The males of other species, such as deer, rabbits, and squirrels, are also called bucks.

carnivores Animals that eat mainly other animals.

carrion The body of a dead animal that is found and eaten by another animal.

cereal crops Crops such as wheat, barley, and corn, which produce grain that is used for food.

colonies Groups of the same type of animal that live together.

doe A female mouse. The females of other animal species, such as deer, rabbits, and squirrels, are also called does.

domestic An animal that is bred as a pet or for food.

dominant The largest, strongest animal of the group.

forage To search for food.

habitat The area where an animal or plant naturally lives.

litter A group of young animals born at the same time from the same mother.

omnivores Animals that eat all types of food, both animal and plants.

predator An animal that kills and eats other animals.

prey Animals that are killed and eaten by predators.

pup A young mouse. Young dogs, seals, and bats are also called pups.

rodents Small animals, such as rats, mice, and voles, with sharp, gnawing teeth.

selective breeding The breeding of different animals together to create a specific characteristic, such as color.

suckle When a mother allows her young to drink milk from her teats.

territory An area that an animal or group of animals defend against others of the same species.

urban A habitat in a town or city.

weaned A young mammal is weaned when it stops taking milk from its mother and eats only solid food.

Finding Out More

Other books to read

Animal Babies: Mammals by Rod Theodorou (Heinemann, 1999)

Animal Classification by Polly Goodman (Hodder Wayland, 2004)

Animal Sanctuary by John Bryant (Open Gate Press, 1999)

Classifying Living Things: Classifying Mammals by Andrew Solway (Heinemann, 2005)

From Egg to Adult: The Life Cycle of Mammals by Mike Unwin (Heinemann, 2003)

Illustrated Encyclopedia of Animals: In Nature and Myth by Fran Pickering (Chrysalis, 2003)

Life Cycles: Cats and Other Mammals by Sally Morgan (Chrysalis, 2001)

Living Nature: Mammals by Angela Royston (Chrysalis, 2005)

My Pet: Rats and Mice by Honor Head (Raintree Steck-Vaughn, 2000)

Outside and Inside: Rats and Mice by Sandra Markle (Atheneum, 2001)

Reading About Mammals by Anna Claybourne (Copper Beech, 2000)

Weird Wildlife: Mammals by Jen Green (Raintree Steck-Vaughn, 2003)

What's the Difference?: Mammals by Stephen Savage (Raintree Steck-Vaughn, 2003)

Web Sites

Due to the changing nature of Internet links, PowerKids Press has developed an online list of Web Sites related to the subject of this book. This site is updated regularly. Please use this link to access this list:
www.powerkidslinks.com/ani/mouse

Index

Page numbers in **bold** refer to a photograph or illustration.